Irene Schindele

CSR in China

A philanthropic response to the Sichuan Earthquake

Social Sciences Series

Impressum / Imprint
Bibliografische Information der Deutschen Nationalbibliothek: Die Deutsche Nationalbibliothek verzeichnet diese Publikation in der Deutschen Nationalbibliografie; detaillierte bibliografische Daten sind im Internet über http://dnb.d-nb.de abrufbar.

Bibliographic information published by the Deutsche Nationalbibliothek: The Deutsche Nationalbibliothek lists this publication in the Deutsche Nationalbibliografie; detailed bibliographic data are available in the Internet at http://dnb.d-nb.de.

Coverbild / Cover image: www.ingimage.com

Verlag / Publisher:
AV Akademikerverlag
ist ein Imprint der / is a trademark of
OmniScriptum GmbH & Co. KG
Heinrich-Böcking-Str. 6-8, 66121 Saarbrücken, Deutschland / Germany
Email: info@akademikerverlag.de

Herstellung: siehe letzte Seite /
Printed at: see last page
ISBN: 978-3-639-48827-2

Table of contents

Introduction

After the accession to the World Trade Organization (WTO) in 2001, anticipated in the late 1970s by the Economic Reform, the awareness of CSR as a relevant matter within the implementation of a business increased steadily in China. Supported in more recent times by the mushrooming of multinational corporations (MNCs), Corporate Social Responsibility practices started to be seen as a fundamental part in doing business and appealing to customers and media, more than as a simple moral commitment.

After the Economic Reform began in 1978, the Chinese government enacted a set of laws addressing environment, consumer and labor force protection. The accession to WTO turned the attention of scholars and media on the matter and give rise to a lot of forums, seminars and associations through entire Mainland China.

In 2008, following the earthquake that hit the province of Sichuan causing 70.000 people to die, both Chinese companies and MNCs helped in the rescue process with donations and active volunteering. According to media and scholars, the occurrence of the earthquake and the following acting of companies changed forever the landscape of CSR in China. The huge media coverage of the issue was not underestimated by international companies, who pursued a CSR policy in line with their international standards, pledging cash or combinations of cash, equipment and services. However, domestic firms' donation exceeded MNCs efforts. A list of so-called Iron roosters appeared on May 14, 2008 circulating on the Internet and by text messages among Chinese people. The term "iron rooster" refers to a bird which has no feathers to give and was therefore related to the stinginess of international firms. Probably fueled by a sense of patriotism, Chinese people strongly supported domestic firms that contributed generously to the rescue process.

"CSR is in many ways the future of public relations in China. Companies would do well to acknowledge this new reality". (Scott Kronick[1])

Chinese CSR however, has developed in a different way and towards different directions than the Western model. Previous research indicates that some factors, for instance cultural principles, historical background, economic development and political setting, can deeply influence the establishment and the perception of a CSR concept in every single land, leading to the creation of different kinds of CSR sensibilities. In China, the peculiar economic growth and the reforms together with cultural concepts have brought to the development of a model of CSR that presents indigenous characteristics which are not to be found in the Western reality. Moreover, social responsibility practices in China differ among private and state-owned companies, due to the long-time difference in role of the two kinds of enterprises.

Goal of this thesis is the analysis of Chinese CSR concepts starting from previous literature and theoretical assumptions, as for instance the implicit/explicit form of CSR hypothesized by Matten and Moon, and looking at the current CSR model keeping in mind the cultural and philosophical concepts which are at the base of the Chinese culture. A famous Chinese petroleum company operating in an international environment has been chosen as example of state-owned enterprise which has, in the years, developed and implemented a CSR model, integrating it into its business.

[1] President of Ogilvy Public Relations Worldwide, China

Aim of the research is to answer the following questions:

Are cultural and historical factors relevant in the creation and development of the Chinese CSR model?

Is it possible, for a Chinese company, to combine the peculiarities of Chinese CSR with the international and Western CSR concepts?

Part I - China National Petroleum Corporation

1.1 The Corporation

The China National Petroleum Corporation (中国石油天然气集团公司, *Zhōngguó Shíyóu Tiānránqì Jítuán Gōngsī)* was founded in 1988 substituting the Ministry of Petroleum Industry of the People's Republic of China, which was in charge for the exploration and development of oil and gas resources in China since 1955. The corporation defines itself as a *"state oil company endowed with certain governmental administrative functions"*. Its headquarters are located in Dongcheng District, Beijing and the company has assets and interests in 29 countries all over the world. CNPC's mission is *"Caring for energy, caring for you"* and *"Energize, Harmonize, Realize"*, expressing its commitment to a harmonious relationship between its business operations and its stakeholders.

"We are committed to protecting the environment and saving resources, promoting the research, development and application of environmentally friendly products, fulfilling our responsibilities to society and promoting development that benefits all"[2].

The vision of the corporation may be summarized as *"Achieving excellence through innovation and integrity"* and matches the main goal of the corporation, which is the creation of an international energy corporation. CNPC aims at developing in a coordinate way its inland and overseas businesses to promote the expansion and exploitation of new energies. CNPC businesses cover the areas of:

- Oil and gas exploration and production, marketing and trading

[2] http://www.cnpc.com.cn/en/aboutcnpc/companyprofile/ourmission/

- Oilfield services in geophysical prospecting
- Oil and gas field surface engineering and pipeline construction
- Manufacturing of prospecting facilities
- Capital management, finance and insurance services
- Unconventional oil and gas resources, biomass energy and other renewable energies.

Currently, CNPC offers different kinds of products and services. Crude oil, natural gas, refined products and chemicals are available for business and customer use[3]. Among others, CNPC runs service stations, shops, car wash, maintenance services, offers car testing, sells fertilizing and lubrication products. The corporation provides moreover the industry with oilfield and engineering services, together with petroleum equipment[4].

The effort towards a harmonious development of the energy sector within China is well expressed through the logo of the corporation. *"The flower-shaped logo's colors are those of China's national flag, with its petals representing our core businesses. The solid red base illustrates CNPC's strength and cohesion as a state-owned enterprise, while the rising sun highlights our brilliant future"*[5].

2008 was a critical year for CNPC, which faced a decrease of 34,9% of total profits, mainly due to an increased special oil gain levy and controls on the refined oil price by the government. 2008 saw moreover a worsening of the overall economic situation and China was hit by snowstorms and by the Sichuan

---

[3] CNPC operates more than 19.000 service stations throughout China

[4] It also provides various chemical products widely used in automotive, building, electronic, textile and pharmaceutical industry.

[5] http://www.cnpc.com.cn/en/aboutcnpc/companyprofile/logo

earthquake[6]. In the following years, however, CNPC managed to recover and stabilize profits.[7]

The same year, CNPC was ranked 25th in Fortune Magazine's top 500 enterprises and fifth among the world's top 50 petroleum companies[8].

1.2 History of the Corporation

The Ministry of Petroleum, CNPC's predecessor, was founded in 1955 and until the late 1980s acquired several commercial oil flows and discovered various oilfields in China. In 1985 the State Council authorized foreign cooperation in specific onshore areas in southern China. On September 17, 1988 the Ministry of Petroleum is dissolved by decision of the State Council and the China National Petroleum Company takes its place. Abundant oil and gas flows are obtained in the Tarim basin in the following years, increasing the power of the newly born corporation. In 1993 begins the first international operation, with the signature of a service contract on an oilfield in Peru. Before the end of 1997, CNPC is working on four oilfields in Sudan and two oilfields in Venezuela. 1998 is a year of changes for CNPC: the Chinese government decides for a reorganization of the corporation and its adjustments to the principle of upstream and downstream integration[9]. Within the framework of the restructuring of CNPC, in 1999 the daughter company PetroChina Company Limited (PetroChina) is founded and listed on the New York Stock Exchange and on the Stock Exchange of Hong Kong. In the following years other subsidiaries are established, among which the China Petroleum Engineering Co.

---

[6] CNPC, Annual Report 2008

[7] Net profit (billion RMB): 149.64 (2007), 91.05 (2008), 87.22(2009), 124.18 (2010), 130.53 (2011)

[8] CNPC, Annual Report 2008

[9] Upstream integration: maximizing the utilization of local inputs, including labour; downstream integration: maximizing local transformation and value addition. Definition by: G. Luciani, Gulf Research Center Foundation, Geneva

in 2001 and BGP Inc. in 2002, optimizing allocation of resources and strengthening the corporation's major operating units. In the same years, CNPC announces purchases of equity in several foreign companies operating in the energy sector. Business operations are expanded in Ecuador, Kazakhstan, Niger, Mauritania, Uzbekistan, Russia, Canada and Middle East countries and new high-yield oilfields are discovered. CNPC launches moreover an ambitious project for the creations of two long-distance gas pipelines across China. On December 23, 2003 a gas blowout occurs at the Luojia H16 in Kaixian County in Chongqing Municipality, killing, poisoning and injuring many surrounding residents[10]. The accident makes the corporation highly aware of the importance of safe operations[11]. Two years later, in November 2005, another major accident occurs, as aniline equipment explodes causing further casualties and environmental pollution. The corporation is urged to implement stricter policies on control and safety.

2008 is a particular year for CNPC: on the one hand the exclusive contract as official partner of the 2008 Beijing Olympics and the recognition by the China Charity Federation for its outstanding contribution to Chinese charities since 2002 improve significantly the image and reputation of the corporation and its subsidiaries, on the other hand the year is studded by adverse economic and natural conditions. The business is severely affected by the snowstorms in southern China and by the Sichuan earthquake and suffers from the newly implemented policies and prices on the petroleum market, causing net profit to sink.

---

[10] PetroChina Company Limited, Announcement on December 31, 2003

[11] http://www.cnpc.com.cn/en/aboutcnpc/companyprofile/history/Major+Events/Major_Events_2003.htm

In the following years net profits increase again and the corporations expand its presence in foreign countries through new acquisition and joint ventures. In 2009 PetroChina, a holding subsidiary of CNPC, becomes parent company of Singapore Petroleum Company Limited and in 2010 it forms a consortium with Total, Petronas and Iraq South Oil Company for a 20-years production service.

CNPC, together with Shell, acquires Australia's Arrow Energy, expanding its overseas operations. The next year, CNPC and Shell sign an agreement for a "cooperation in Canadian oil sands development, unconventional natural gas and oilfield services"[12].

1.3 Strategy

The corporation's strategy is expressed though three points:

- Maximize and diversify resources while maintaining the domestic leadership
- Maximize profits and obtain dominant position through economies of scale
- Enhance international cooperation and expand international oil trade

Through the establishment of several subsidiaries, CNPC is seeking the best allocation of its assets and resources. The division and distribution of tasks and businesses among subsidiaries has proved itself to be an efficient way for exploiting strategic advantages and core competencies. PetroChina International, for instance, is responsible for CNPC's international trading activities, whereas six specialized equipment manufacturing companies take care of the manufacturing business according to a quality assurance system and

[12] CNPC, Annual Report 2011

international certifications[13]. The businesses of asset management, financing and insurance, acquisition and merger as well as investment and management are carried out by CNPC's subsidiary CNPC Asset Management Co. and its holding subsidiary China Petroleum Finance Co, Ltd. Sticking to the concept of *"mutual benefit and win-win for common development"*, in the last years CNPC has started several joint ventures with both Chinese and foreign companies, all developed by the subsidiary CNPC Exploration & Development Company. Among them, joint ventures have been undertaken with ASSICURAZIONI GENERALI for the insurance business, with ONGC, an Indian oil company, for the control of Syrian pipelines and with Shell and Qatar for the creation of refineries in various countries.[14] Joint ventures have mainly two goals: on the one hand, they are a way of splitting businesses and competencies other than subsidiaries and on the other they allow a rapid expansion in new countries and markets, granting access to greater resources while sharing risks with partners.

1.4 CNPC Corporate Social Responsibility

Both in the missions and in the vision, CNPC expresses its commitment for a harmonious development of its business within the society and the environment. The corporation stresses its willingness of creating positive *"relationships between operation and safety, energy and the environment, and corporate and community interests"*.

CNPC's sustainable development model is made up by three basic factors that are economic growth, environment protection and social development. A proper interaction among them is the key for a successful business.

---

[13] ISO 9000, ISO 14000 and ISO 10012

[14] http://www.alarabiya.net/articles/2011/10/13/171616.html

The corporation identifies seven different kinds of stakeholders: government, to whom the company should grant a stable market supply, shareholders, which are interested in maximizing profits, employees, clients and consumers, business partners, related institutions and communities.

Since 2006, when the new Company Law was enacted, the corporation has been publishing annual CSR reports according to the guidelines of Global Reporting Initiative (GRI)[15] and of the Oil and Gas Industry Guidance on Voluntary Sustainability Reporting jointly issued by IPIECA and API[16].
During the years the corporation and its subsidiaries have been awarded several prizes for their corporate social responsibility practices in the areas of;

- environmental protection
- safety and health
- social contribution[17].

1.4.1 Environmental Protection

Environmental protection is nowadays a fundamental aspect of corporate social responsibility policies, even more for a company playing in the petroleum market. CNPC takes care in particular of energy saving and emissions reduction. The parent group urges its subsidiaries into using environment management systems, pollutant discharge-reduction index systems, monitoring systems and appraisal systems. Recently, CNPC has become involved in the project of the

[15] GRI is a non-profit organization that promotes economic, environmental and social sustainability. Website: https://www.globalreporting.org
[16] Available at http://www.api.org/environment-health-and-safety/environmental-performance/corporate-reporting/oil-gas-industry-guidance.aspx
[17] The first three aspects express the acceptance by the corporation of the HSE system, which is an international standard, whereas the last point is more linked to Chinese standards.

China National Energy Administration (CNEA), which founded the Aviation Fuel Steering Committee and Clean Transport Workgroup to promote the sustainable development of China's aviation biofuel industry. On May 26, 2010 CNPC signed a contract of cooperation with Air China, Boeing and Honeywell's UOP. CNPC takes charge of supplying the aviation biofuel needed by the test flights[18]. The first test flight of a passenger plane took place in October 2011 and succeeded. Aviation Biofuel produces 50-90% less greenhouse gas than traditional kerosene.

CNPC publicize furthermore its attention and care for the foreign areas it is going to exploit. The joint venture between CNPC and Sinopec called Andes Petroleum for instance, operating in tropical rainforests in northeastern Ecuador, uses 3D seismic exploration technology to avoid damages to the rainforest and, in the attempt of protecting biodiversity, it has always drilled new wells in old well sites. The company has adopted European or US environmental protection policies. As a result, CNPC Andes Petroleum was awarded, among others, the World Oil HSE/Sustainable Development award[19].

In 2008 seven new technologic innovations of the corporation, including "Heavy Oil Wastewater Recycling and its Application" won National Awards for Science and Technology and the corporation launched the Liaoyang Petrochemical N2O Emission Reduction Project, which could cut down emissions by over 12 million tons, "about 10% of national emission reduction volume"[20]. It is the first large-scale Clean Development Mechanism (CDM) project in China.

---

[18] Successful Trial Flight of Aviation Biofuel http://www.cnpc.com.cn/en/environmentsociety/environment/case/

[19] Information available at http://www.andespetro.com, Annual and CSR reports

[20] CNPC, Corporate Social Responsibility Report 2008

1.4.2 Safety and health

CNPC considers its employees its best asset. Safety and health are of greatest importance in CSR policies of the corporation, as oil industry presents high risk rates. A "Safety and Environmental Protection Year" campaign was launched for four consecutive years, centered on human-oriented safety principles.

The company refers to the HSE Management System for strengthening health and safety policies. This system uses a PDCA management model, consisting of planning, doing, checking and action processes. It is composed by seven key elements, that are commitment, guidelines, planning, organization and resources and documents, implementation, checking and correction, and assessment. The interaction of all elements should bring to a continuously upgrading system[21].

Safety is intended both toward employees and toward environment. Operational safety is achieved through different management systems formulated according to international, national and corporation standards. In 2008 in particular, the corporation organized a number of activities that took place during the Beijing Olympic Games. Its major subsidiaries and areas were inspected to ensure that no safety accident could occur. The total investment into safety risk management reached the amount of 33.977 billion RMB and safety conditions dramatically improved. *"Throughout the year, no major fatality, fire or explosion accidents due to industrial production occurred"*[22].

[21] CNPC, Corporate Social Responsibility Report, 2007
[22] CNPC, Corporate Social Responsibility Report 2008

Moreover, a strict emergency response plan has been issued in the last years, which is completed through 18 specialized plans for all eventualities. The core concepts are forecasting, early warning and rapid response.

The monitoring of occupational health and occupational disease hazards has been strengthened and on-site healthcare services to better safeguard oilfield and pipeline workers' health. In Sudan a CNPC-SOS clinic was set up to provide emergency rescue training and first aid courses to the local employees.

An Employee Assistance Program (EAP) was moreover adopted in 2008, to provide staff with psychological help and support, to ease pressure and bad mood and "enable them to work with a good psychological status and experience the joy of work"[23].

Safety is also expressed through quality. In an effort of improving the quality of finished products and engineering services, CNPC is developing its existing quality management system. The majority of CNPC subsidiaries and joint venture is implementing advanced quality management systems and almost all member companies' practices have been officially certified and tested.

1.4.3 Social Contribution

CNPC divides its contribution to public welfare in different areas:

- Education
- Local development
- Sport sponsorship
- Science and culture
- Disaster relief

[23] CNPC, Corporate Social Responsibility Report 2008

Contributions to public welfare are made according to international standards through donations, infrastructure building and in-kind donations. However, the corporation is strongly supporting and encouraging volunteering and voluntary donations by its employees as a form of collectivism, proving founded the fact that Chinese corporate social responsibility may assume different characteristics and priorities from the western practices.

CNPC considers the efforts towards education a traditional virtue of Chinese people. The corporation has got involved in several activities such as the "Hope Project", building so-called Hope Schools all over China, the "Spring Rain Project" and the "Oasis Action" with the aim of helping children living in poverty in continuing their education. Moreover, in year 2001 CNPC established CNPC Scholarships for outstanding college students, which are distributed among seven petroleum and petrochemical colleges and fifteen universities. In 2008, CNPC's donations to education reached 140 million RMB[24] (US$20.136.100).

The concept of local development is strictly linked, or better, matches perfectly, the principle of "mutually beneficial for common development". The corporation aims at creating positive relationships with the communities it gets in touch with and pursues a shared welfare. In every kind of business, the respect of local customs is set as priority for CNPC. The corporation tries to improve local facilities[25] through donations, voluntary service and infrastructure construction. In this way, CNPC contributes to the local economic and social betterment. As an example, in 2007 the company offered 38 million RMB (US$5.465.510), partly collected through voluntary employees' donations, to buy 19 channels on China Central Television (CCT) and 10 provincial TV station, "to broadcast free

[24] CNPC, Corporate Social Responsibility Report 2008
[25] Transport, healthcare, education, job opportunities

advertising for businesses in 100 poverty-stricken counties across the country"[26]. The project responded to the solicitation of the central government to build a "new socialist countryside".

Another case study proposed by the corporation regarding its commitment to local commitment concerns Andes Petroleum, a joint venture of CNPC and Sinopec. Andes Petroleum is one of the biggest foreign oil companies operating in Ecuador. Since it started its business in early 2006, the company has faced several challenges, among which cultural clashes, ethnic conflicts and a degeneration of public security. As a response, the company has launched several projects, including the Andes Cocoa Garden, a mobile medical team, school buses and an employment program. Moreover, planting techniques have been taught to local farmers and financial support has been given to public services.

Since 2005 the corporation is actively sponsoring sport events and activities. It all started with the ninth National Badminton Tournament for College Students, in which participated more than 400 participants from many universities around China. The event was sponsored by PetroChina Lubricant Company. In the same year CNPC signed an agreement and became official partner of the Beijing Olympic Games as exclusive energy supplier for all competition areas. "Our company was the sole sponsor of this ceremony, the first example of a company co-organizing and Olympic cultural event. We made full use of the opportunity of working with the Beijing Olympics to demonstrate our corporate values and high-quality service"[27].

[26] CNPC Case Study, Building an Information Platform to Promote Rural Development. Available at: http://www.cnpc.com.cn/en/environmentsociety/public/case/Building_an_information_platform_to_promote_rural_development.htm

[27] http://www.cnpc.com.cn/en/environmentsociety/public/sports/

Concerning science and culture, CNPC sponsored in December 2004 an expedition in the South Pole. The 21st Chinese South Pole Exploration Team was offered 15 million RMB (US$2.157.440) by the CNPC PetroChina Lubricant Company. In addition, CNPC covered all expenses of fuel for the vehicles needed. In 2005 CNPC sponsored "Fairytales Painted by Children", an exhibition of children's works held at the National Art Museum of China in Beijing.

Disaster relief is a priority among CSR practices for Chinese enterprises. The beneficiaries are not only Chinese companies, but countries all around the globe. In 2004, in response to the Indian Ocean Tsunami, CNPC staff collected 12.57 million RMB (approx. US$1.800.000) to be donated to the coastal countries through the Red Cross Society and further US$650.000 were sent by overseas subsidiaries. In year 2006 the corporation helped the Sichuan Province to fight a severe loss of crops and shortage of drinking water due to continuously high temperatures and drought, donating 10 million RMB. The following year CNPC's total donations amounted to 124 million RMB (US$17.834.800). 2008 saw the Sichuan earthquake, snowstorms in southern China and a tropic storm in Myanmar. CNPC supported both economically and practically the rescue efforts in all three disasters. US$300.000 were donated to Myanmar's Department of Energy, 14 million RMB (approx. US$2.000.000) to snowstorm-stricken provinces. For both occurrences, total employees donation exceeded 51 million RMB (US$7.335.290).

1.5 CNPC and the Sichuan Earthquake

The earthquake caused severe damage to CNPC's production facilities in the hit areas like Sichuan, Chongqing, Shaanxi and Gansu, leading to heavy losses for the business. More than 50 companies operating in the quake-hit province had to suspend operations and 38 stations were completely destroyed. Furthermore, 10 CNPC staff member were killed in the disaster and 23,000 employees and their families lost home.

As reported in a news release of May, 15, the day after the earthquake CNPC established a team in charge for the relief efforts headed by the President Jiang Jiemin, who visited the affected areas one week after the disaster. The same release included 4 major disposition to be undertaken immediately by the corporation, that were

- inspecting oil and gas pipelines, oil stores and service stations in the hit areas, with particular emphasis on the consequences and safety risks caused by the earthquake
- providing 100,000 tons of refined oil as a support for relief operations
- giving priority to saving people
- a first donation of 10 million RMB (approx. US$1.440.000) and mobilization of CNPC's professional resources to provide support.

The same day a team of CNPC's staff left for the quake hit-regions and 22 hours after the disaster the pipeline in Chengdu was restarted and provided oil supplies to the relief works[28]. CNPC publicized moreover its interest in cooperating actively with local governments *"to assist people affected by the disaster, enhance safety management and anti-terrorist works in key sections*

[28] CNPC, News release, May 15, 2008. Available at: http://www.cnpc.com.cn/en/press/newsreleases/2008/5-15.htm

and critical facilities, and reinforce security management in mining communities in quake-hit areas to ensure social stability"[29].

With the intention of coordinating and unify relief operations, CNPC established the Petroleum Enterprise Coordination Group and Emergency Headquarters of Sichuan and Chongqing Region, which made reports to the government of Sichuan.

CNPC subsidiaries that suffered from the quake were force by headquarters to restore their operations as soon as possible and help the "Fuel for Life" project in order to provide oil supply. More than 105.000 tons of oil products, aviation fuel and diesel were carried by means of tankers despite the aftershocks. The corporation and its daughter companies, moreover, sent material aid as tents, mechanical equipment and vehicles, valued in more than 1 million RMB.

Some experts from the CNPC Central Hospital were sent to the quake-hit provinces, together with staff members of the epidemic prevention station of Liaohe Oilfield. Their task was to introduce epidemic prevention methods and first-aid practices.

On May, 16 CNPC announced a further donation of 13 million RMB (approx. US$1.870.000), 10 of which to be divided among the provinces and 3 destined to the Dongfang Electric Corporation, severely affected by the earthquake[30].

The corporation stressed moreover the importance of employees' donations and by May 18, one week after the quake, the total amount reached 80 million RMB (US$11.500.000). Donations were made from employees of CNPC's

[29] CNPC, News release, May 16, 2008. Available at: http://www.cnpc.com.cn/en/press/newsreleases/2008/5-16-3.htm
[30] CNPC, News release, May 16, 2008. Available at: http://www.cnpc.com.cn/en/press/newsreleases/2008/5-16-6.htm

subsidiaries all over the world and from main partners' too. In order to help children and schools of the hit provinces, the corporation launched the project "Action of One Million CNPC Staff to Donate for the Reconstruction of one hundred Schools". Besides, employees contributed by paying voluntary special membership fee for disaster relief.

As reported in the 2008 CSR report:

"By the end of 2008, CNPC and its employees had donated money and materials equivalent to RMB 343 million[31] *to the earthquake-stricken area"*[32].

The relief efforts undertaken by CNPC were highly praised by both central and local governments. In October 2008, at the National Earthquake Relief Summary and Award Meeting, a great number of staff members and projects of CNPC were honored and the subsidiary CNPC Sichuan Marketing Company won the "National Earthquake Relief Hero Collective" title, assigned by the State Council and the Central Military Commission.

[31] Approx. US$49.300.000
[32] CNPC, Corporate Social Responsibility Report 2008

Part II - Corporate Social Responsibility

2.1 General Overview

The concept of Corporate Social Responsibility (CSR) was first broached in the 1920s by Oliver Sheldon, director of an English confectionery company. He argued that basic economic needs and social needs are on the same level of importance in doing business. In the late 1970s and early 1980s the issue was on the rise as corporations started to be faced with public opinion and CSR began to be seen as a way of improving the image of the company. However, a universal definition of corporate social responsibility has never been given. In 2006, McWilliams concluded that *"...there is a no strong consensus on a definition for CSR".* According to Matten and Moon (2008), this difficulty in defining CSR may be derived from the fact that *"CSR is an umbrella term overlapping with some, and being synonymous with other, conceptions of business-society relations".*
The World Business Council for Sustainable Development (WBCSD) defined corporate social responsibility as *"the continuing commitment by business to behave ethically and contribute to economic development while improving the quality of life of the workforce and their families as well as of the community and society at large"*[33].

All definitions up to nowadays have been presented within Carroll's (1979, 1991) framework. Carroll defined CSR as a model built up by four dimensions in which economic responsibilities are consistent with maximizing profits for shareholders, legal responsibilities force the company to comply with governmental laws and

[33] World Business Council for Sustainable Development, *Corporate Social Responsibility*, p.3. Retrieved from http://www.wbcsd.org

ethical responsibilities indicate the company the standards considered fair by the society. The fourth dimension is philanthropy and according to Wood (1991) it is *"the domain of discretionary responsibility"*. Ramasamy *et al.* (2008) described Carroll's CSR model as a pyramid in which the basic responsibilities as economic and legal ones are at the base, while more sophisticated responsibilities as ethical and philanthropic ones are at the pinnacle. The pyramid form implies that the advanced responsibilities are supported by the basic ones. The interdependence of responsibilities was also expressed in the definition of CSR given in 1971 by the Committee for Economic Development (CED), which referred to three concentric circles of responsibilities:

"The inner circle includes the clear-cut basic responsibilities for the efficient execution of the economic function – products, jobs, and economic growth. The intermediate circle encompasses responsibilities to exercise this economic function with a sensitive awareness of changing social values and priorities: for example, with respect to environmental conservation; hiring and relations with employees ... The outer circle outlines newly emerging and still amorphous responsibilities that business should assume to become more broadly involved in actively improving the social environment. Society is beginning to turn to corporations for help with major social problems such as poverty and urban blight."[34]

In current CSR research, Carroll's model has been adopted together with Freeman's (1984) stakeholder approach, which defines who the corporation should be responsible for. Stakeholders are *"any group or individual who can affect, or is affected by, the achievement of a corporation's purpose"*. Employees, customers, suppliers, shareholders, governments, competitors and

[34] Committee for Economic Development, *Social responsibilities of business corporations*, 1971

communities are generally the representative groups of stakeholders. The largest stakeholder group, *i.e.* consumers, has gathered an incredible power towards firms' decisions and profits in recent years. Research indicates that "*a combination of more product choices, wealth, education and brand consciousness*" together with an increased availability of ethical products has led to a more socially conscious consumer[35]. Managers have therefore realized that CSR is not only an ethical or philosophical obligation, but also an economic and profit-enhancing opportunity.

2.2 CSR Across Countries

Research and empirical evidence suggest that CSR practices and dimensions vary a lot among different countries. Matten and Moon (2008) argue that these differences derive from a *"variety of longstanding, historically entrenched institutions"*.

As institutions are meant not only formal and physical institutions like government or corporations, but also rules, laws and incentives. According to Huntington (1969), institutions are *"stable, valued recurring patterns of behavior"*, which possibly enable foreseeable interactions. Institutions are reflected in the way societies develop different market systems, together with ethic and social principles. As a consequence, Matten and Moon argue that differences are to be expected in CSR practices and policies among different societies. They argue that differences across countries are linked to historically grown institutional structures. They distinguish four key points in historically grown institutional structures: political system, financial system, education and labor system and

[35] Ramasamy et al. (2008)

the cultural system. All these factors together determine the nature of firms operating in the market, the organization of the market and the coordination and control systems. Regarding the nature of the firm, the institutional structure defines the control of private hierarchies over economic processes or the degree of freedom allowed to managers.

The organization of the market is defined by institutional structure at the level of cooperation and economic relations between actors on the market, as the influence of business associations, the role of personal relations or the extent of cooperation between firms. The last factor defined by institutional structure is the coordination and control system, intended as the way in which corporations are governed.

An attentive analysis of all factors together allows determining the nature of elements of CSR, divided into explicit and implicit elements. Explicit CSR refers to *"corporate policies that assume and articulate responsibility for some societal interests"*[36]. Explicit CSR is usually identified in voluntary programs as disaster relief and may involve cooperation with governmental and nongovernmental organizations.

Implicit CSR, on the contrary, refers to the role corporation play within the formal and informal institutions toward community's interests. It is normally made up of rules and values that *"result in requirement for corporations to address stakeholder issues and that define proper obligations of corporate actors in collective rather than individual terms"*[37].

---

[36] Matten and Moon, (2008), p. 409

[37] Matten and Moon (2008), p.409. Table 1, p.501

FIGURE 1
Implicit and Explicit CSR

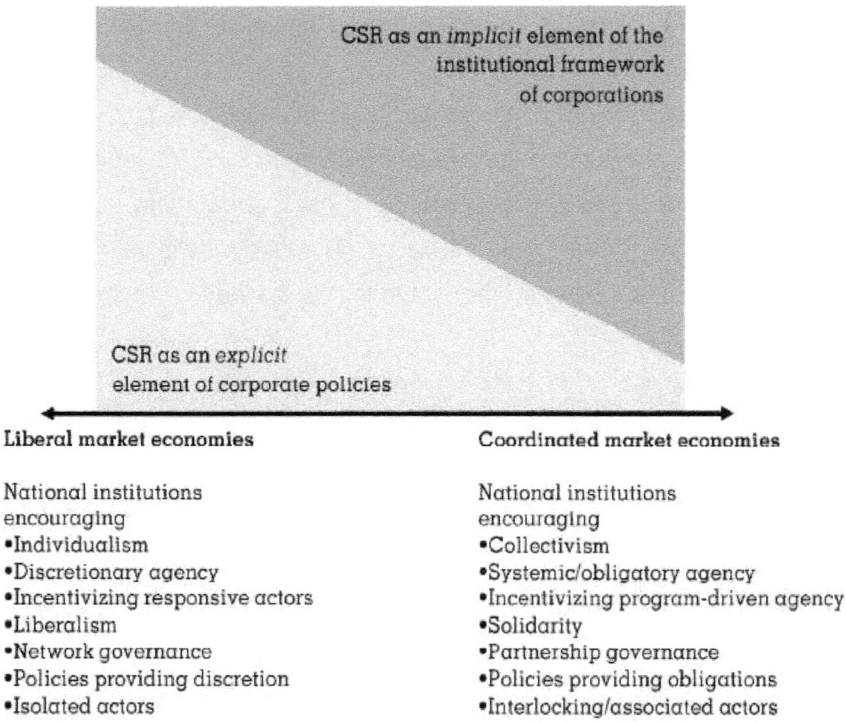

Matten and Moon applied this analysis to CSR practices in the United States and in Europe, drawing the conclusion that United States present explicit CSR elements whereas Europe historically presents more implicit ones. The analysis proposed by Matten and Mood is enforceable also on other countries, as institutions determining explicit or implicit CSR elements are to be found in every society under different forms. According to the authors, explicit CSR is going to spread in the developing world among societies with weak institutions and poor governance mechanisms, whereas countries like China or Russia are likely to develop implicit CSR elements, as they have always been influenced by a greater governmental presence and stronger regulations.

2.3 China's Economic Revolution, SOEs reform and Globalization

China's economy prior to 1949 can be characterized as a land-scarce but labor-abundant economy being drawn into contact with an industrializing west. In 1949 the People's Republic of China was settled, and a strong economic development started. Five-year plans were implemented starting in 1953, affecting different areas of the economy, and in 1958 the Great Leap Forward plan was executed. The GLF however, while boosting dramatically the heavy industry sector, led to a decrease of overall living conditions, bringing almost 30 million people to starve. Between 1966 and 1976 the cultural revolution took place, preached by Mao Tse-Tung, aiming at enforcing the socialist principles against the growing capitalism of Western countries. Since 1978 till nowadays a further economic reform has been implemented, orienting outward the economy and introducing capitalist market principles. The reform was the result of a set of factors: among them, the failure of the cultural revolution, the understanding by part of officials of the shortcomings of the planned economy and the successful economic development in other parts of Asia[38]. The reform was carried out in three phases: firstly, micromanagement institution were transformed (the household responsibility system was implemented, by which managers are responsible for the enterprise's losses and profits), secondly the resource allocation mechanism was modified (in the areas of material management, foreign trade and financial system) and lastly the macro policy environment was

[38] Four Little Dragons (Japan and South Korea, Singapore, Hong Kong, Taiwan)

reformed, with changes in the policies regarding price, foreign exchanges and interest rates setting. The reform was a bottom-up process, following the concept of Gradualism[39]: policies were adopted through experiments in an easy-to-hard sequence, and transitional costs were spread over long periods, resulting in an economically and politically more feasible transformation. As Deng Xiaoping said, the reform implementation followed the Chinese philosophy of *"crossing the river by feeling the stones, 摸着石头过河"*.

The reform proved itself to be successful, as it led to a high-speed economic growth[40] and to improvements in economic incentives and efficiency. After the first decollectivization of agriculture and the opening to foreign investments, a second stage of reform was needed: the reform of State Owned Enterprises (SOEs).

The rapid growth in industrial output since 1978 was closely linked to the enterprise system. The major sources of industrial growth were the development of a non-state economy[41], the opening to foreign invested enterprises[42] and the reform of SOEs. With the economic reform and the creation of a non-state economy, in fact, SOEs had to face a greater challenge and, for the first time, market competition. Before the reform state-owned enterprises were completely owned by the state[43] and directly managed by the governments at various levels and sort of monopolies in specific sectors had been created. The reform, started in the early 1990s, aimed at increasing the autonomy of SOEs and meeting the challenge of non-state economy. For this purpose, it was necessary to boost

[39] Opposite to Big Bang Theory
[40] Average annual growth rate (1978-2008): 9.3%
[41] That was the major contributor to the economic growth since the reform
[42] Mainly owned by investors from Hong Kong, Macau and Taiwan
[43] The government, in a planned economy, is the principal subject who takes centralized decisions about the allocation of resources

motivation, improve the utilization of resources and reestablish a market-oriented mechanism in doing business. The reform introduced a profit retention system, the expansion of managerial discretion and a responsibility system. The vitality of SOEs was enhanced through a simplified administrative control and a reform of the taxation system and mandatory plans were reduced. SOEs managers were given higher discretion in marketing, pricing, purchasing, self-financing and many other areas of business. Moreover, the expansion of market competition and the advanced techniques and management systems of non-state companies[44] spread into SOEs[45].

In 1993 the CPC central committee wrote a plan regarding the establishment of a socialist market economic system that aimed at the corporatization of the state-owned economy. Several SOEs turned into shareholding limited companies and the government chose to retain control over the bigger ones in the sectors of electric power, coal, petroleum, chemicals, rail system, air and water transportation system, telecommunications, finance and banking.

The reform, however, is still not over. In recent years the so-called "SOEs jam" has drawn the attention of economic planners and researchers: SOEs have to compete in the market as any other market entity, but they are subject to heavy policy burdens. As government agents, indeed, SOEs shoulder the responsibility of paying workers' pensions, social welfare expenses and layoff living subsidies. In 1998 pension payment for retired workers made up 25% of the enterprises' total salary payments. Furthermore, overstaffing and unemployment began to emerge as the reform went on, being a great disadvantage for SOEs in the market-oriented economy. For this reason, in the last years many sectors were

[44] Foreign invested companies in particular
[45] Experts defined it as a learning/spill-over effect.

subject to further reforms which aimed at eliminating policy burdens and welfare costs.

Since the economic reform China has opened up and started a process of globalization. A significant step was taken in 1986, when China officially applied for the membership in the World Trade Organization (WTO) and in 2001, when China was finally admitted. The WTO, founded in 1995 following the General Agreement on Tariff and Trade (GATT) established in the wake of the Second World War, is a global international organization dealing with the rules of trade between nations. At its heart there are the WTO agreements, negotiated and signed by the member nations and ratified by the countries' parliaments.

Globalization has led to severe changes in the Chinese economic and institutional landscape. China has adapted not only to foreign technology and foreign corporate management techniques, but also to foreign institutions and practices, as accounting standards, reporting, security laws, a central bank structure and western concept of rules and law. Shen (2009) defines economic globalization as *"an evolutionary process of integration of world markets, characterized by liberalizing economic activities, investment and trade, free flow of production and management factors"*[46]. The globalization process results in a convergence of different countries' policies regulating market participants. Shen argues that in the case of corporate social responsibility, *"convergence is a product of social development"*, that is a sign both of social productivity growth and of social progress and civilization.

However, as already stated, institutions cannot be perfectly similar among countries and therefore Shen's convergence of CSR tends to resemble, rather than to be identical among societies. Different social developing stages, different

[46] Shen et al. (2009), p. 134

organizational structures, different levels of productivity growth and different cultural and historical backgrounds all together modify CSR elements across countries. Globalization has brought nations to share a common understanding of CSR, but every country has developed its own particular CSR system.

2.4 CSR Concepts In China

As asserted by Matten and Moon, China has always been characterized by a strong presence of government, both on markets and companies' businesses as well as on culture. Chinese CSR (公司社会责任, Gōngsī shèhuì zérèn) is therefore supposed to present implicit elements and the institutional structure should encourage collectivism and solidarity. Matten and Mood affirm that according to results Chinese CSR should be subject to law and regulations, as set by the implicit form of CSR. And so it actually is. In China, CSR is completely controlled through laws and regulations. The most general provision is set by the article 5 of the new Company Law, issued in 2006[47]. Further regulations are to be found in the "Consumer Protection Act", in the "National Responsible Competitiveness Act", "Contract Law", "Labor Law of the People's Republic of China", "Trade Union Law of the People's Republic of China" and many others. Moreover, CSR principles are being promulgated among SOEs through public governmental[48] and private initiatives, such as the Responsible Supply Chain Association and the joint declarations about CSR Industrial Principles by

[47] Article 5: When undertaking business operations, a company shall comply with the laws and administrative regulations, social morality and business morality. It shall act in good faith, accept the supervision of the government and the general public, and bear social responsibilities.

[48] CSR Guideline for State-Owned Enterprises (SOE) by State-owned Assets Supervision and Administration Commission (SASAC), PR China. Available at: http://www.syntao.com/E_Page_Show.asp?Page_ID=6407

industrial associations. Listed companies are furthermore subject to the CSR guidelines issued by the Shenzhen stock exchange since 2006 [49]. This differentiates Chinese CSR concepts from the countries that present explicit CSR elements as the United States, in which CSR assumes a more voluntary role.

In Western countries CSR dimensions have been object of research since the 1970s and countless models have been constructed. Among them, Carroll's included economic, legal, ethical and discretionary responsibilities, whereas Gallo (2004) divided CSR concepts as following: *"providing satisfactory services to the society, creating economic wealth, boosting overall development of internal corporate personnel and ensuring sustainable corporate development"*[50]. Xu *et al.* (2009) summarized all dimensions derived from previous research with the help of a survey undertaken in year 2006 by the World Bank and the Peking University based on 1268 industrial enterprises throughout China. Eliminating redundancies among previous studies, eight dimensions of western CSR were found: economic responsibility, legal responsibility, environmental protection, consumerism, shareholder interest, employment development, equality and social donation/charitable causes. The same analysis was then conducted on Chinese companies, deriving nine CSR dimensions. The research indicates both common and unique dimensions. As the table 2 shows, Chinese CSR differentiates itself as it does not include the two major dimensions of shareholder interests and equality and presents the unique dimensions of good faith, employment, social stability and progress.

---

[49] Available at http://www.szse.cn/main/en/RulesandRegulations/SZSERules/GeneralRules/10636.shtml

[50] Xu et al (2010), p. 326

Western unique CSR dimensions	Chinese unique CSR dimensions
Shareholders Create profits Information transparency Protect interests of small and medium shareholders Improve governance structure *Equality* Racial equality Gender equality Equal opportunities	*Good faith* Comply with business ethics Operate in good faith, honor contracts *Employment* Increase job opportunities Reemploy lay-offs Ease national employment pressure Provide jobs for the disabled *Social stability and progress* Ensure social stability Promote social progress Patriotism, promote national prosperity

Whereas there is no need of explaining western dimensions and common dimensions between Chinese and western CSR, the unique characteristics demand a more detailed analysis. Good faith requires companies to operate in good faith, honoring obligations and contracts and *"provide genuine goods at fair prices"*[51]. Good faith is expressly preached by the fifth article of the New Company previously examined. These requirements are similar to Carroll's ethical responsibility but "good faith" has never been recognized among western CSR practices. The second dimension is employment and is strictly linked with China's peculiar development stage and background. Companies are required

[51] Xu et al, (2010). p. 330

to provide as many job opportunities as possible in order to ease employment pressure. This involvement by corporations is a response to the increasing issue of unemployment in China and reflects the attention that the matter has received after the reconstructing of SOEs that led to a massive number of lay-offs. The last unique characteristic, social stability and progress, is probably rooted in the Confucian philosophy of ensuring social stability and harmony and boosting patriotism.

2.5 Chinese culture principles influencing CSR practices

2.5.1 Confucianism

Confucianism is the cornerstone of traditional Chinese culture. Originated more than 2000 years ago, it started as an ethical and philosophical system preached by Confucius (孔夫子). At the base of the ideology is humanism, intended as care towards the human being. Confucius believed that individuals, family, peace and prosperity of state and the foundation of stability were at the roots of social relations (Yao, 2000).As Yao asserted, Confucianism was developed around two central theses: *"that goodness can be taught and learned, and that society can only be in harmony an at peace under the guidance of wisdom".* Confucianism preaches the five principles of *ren* (仁), which forces the individual to altruism within a community, *yi* (義), which is the pursue of justice, *li* (禮), that is a set of norms in order to act properly within a community, *zhi* (智), which is learning from others for the betterment of the individual, and *xin* (信), that is integrity and good sense in everyday actions. Is quite obvious that Confucianism principles resemble some CSR aspects, in particular *ren,* which urges a taking-giving relation between the single actors and the whole community. According to

Zhu and Yao (2008), *"to some extent, the value of Confucian culture has invisibly formed the fundamental sources of modern CSR as an earlier ethical element".* The core concept of CSR of caring about community's interests is at the base of Confucianism too and the harmony between individual/enterprise and community/society preached by the ancient doctrine is a pillar in the CSR statements of many Chinese enterprises (see CNPC). Zhu and Yao therefore assert that *"the modern value of CSR has to some extent been developed and promoted on the basis of researchers having partially absorbed Japanese and Chinese Eastern cultures which both belong to the cycle of Confucian culture integrated with Western cultures"*. They furthermore underline the fact that an *"the value of collective concern or harmonious competition advocated in the Confucian cultural value has a role of compensation and correction on the value of individual concern or fatal competition advocated in some Western cultures",* implying that CSR practices in China are the result of different and opposite elements coming together and that a proper combination should be reached in order to regulate both domestic and foreign business relations.

2.5.2 Guanxi Theory

Guanxi, that is "social relations" or "personal relations", is the center of Chinese culture and public relations practices – therefore the concept receives greater importance in businesses too. Yang and Wang (2011) have studied *guanxi* as a governance mechanism in business markets and argue that "*to develop guanxi is to form the basis for a gradual transition from being considered an outsider, as opposed to an insider, so that a long-term close relationship can be established and developed".* This depends mostly by reciprocal feeling among two parties and is determined through three key factors: "*qing* (emotion or feeling), *li* (reciprocity) and *liyi* (utilitarian benefits)". As asserted by Fang (2010), "*the unique guanxi feature of the Chinese culture poses challenges for western businesses*". A well-developed *guanxi* in years of business activity may be a precious resource in case of need, as it increases the likelihood of receiving assistance and the creation of cooperation. Multinational corporations, on their side, may encounter problems in entering Chinese markets with *guanxi*.

2.5.3 Mianzi

Mianzi, 面子, literally face, is a feature deeply rooted in the Chinese culture. It indicates the reputation, self-respect and prestige that an individual has within a community. *Mianzi* applies to individuals as well as to society or to the country in general. A Chinese saying affirms that "*Face is as important to a man as a bark is to a tree*" (Fang, 2010). According to research, *mianzi* explains why it is common in China to make lists of top students or top enterprises (see Iron Roosters).

2.5.4 High-context

Opposite to low-context, high-context cultures tend to spread more indirect messages than explicit messages. The difference between high and low-context, theorized by anthropologist Edward T. Hall in 1976, differentiates the two kinds of cultures by how messages are delivered. In a low-context culture, messages are more explicit and single words are not of fundamental importance, whereas in high-context societies messages are often spread in an implicit way and few words can communicate a complex message. According to Fang (2010), *"individuals raised in high-context cultures tend to depend on the context of messages, such as circumstances and settings, speaker's social statuses and positions, timing and the way messages are surveyed"*. Consequently, western nations are identified as low-context nations, while Asian countries are examples of high-context cultures. This reflects on the way businesses and enterprises open to society, through acting and active participation but also through reports, CSR declaration, disclosures and new releases.

2.5.5 Collectivism

Fang identifies collectivism as a further feature of Chinese culture. Collectivistic cultures are opposite to individualistic ones. Individuals embracing collectivism put greater importance on group goals rather than on individual success and stress the importance of cohesion and interdependence among social groups. Collectivism, in particular if intended as social cohesion among socially equal subjects, has often been associated with socialism.

2.5.6 Out-group bias

Ma (2010) identifies out-group bias as another feature of Chinese culture. The phenomenon, known as intergroup bias too, *"refers to the tendency to evaluate one's own group or group members (the in-groups) more favorably than groups to which one does not belong and their members (the out-groups)"* [52]. Collectivistic societies usually presents more out-group bias, meaning that individuals raised in collectivistic communities tend to be more competitive and less "friendly" when dealing with members of out-groups . Individualistic individuals, on the contrary, differentiate less among in or out-groups and therefore have a similar attitude towards the two different groups. In the context of business-making, negotiators from collectivistic cultures are more likely to use

[52] Ma (2010), p.125

more competitive and *"ethically questionable strategies"*[53] towards competitors, in order to protect the interests of the in-group members. Ma argues therefore that *"collectivists will change their perceived appropriateness of certain negotiation strategies according to who they are dealing with".*

2.6 SOEs Corporate Responsibility Practices and Regulation

According to Lin (2010), in the Chinese context the concept of CSR is easily confused with "*the idea of state-owned enterprises as social services and benefits providers (企业办社会, Qǐyè bàn shèhuì)"*[54]. Prior to the reform, SOEs were both business units and social service providers, which had to grant a standard welfare to their employees and communities in which they were operating. In the past, moreover, SOEs were in charge of educational and health care institutions, pensions and many more services. This structure is blamed as one of the causes of the inefficiency of SOEs.

Lin (2010) identifies some important differences between CSR and *Qǐyè bàn shèhuì:* as a first aspect, CSR in China is the result of modern globalization, whereas the second concept is an "*old economic model operated in the traditional Chinese communism*"; secondly, stakeholder groups vary consistently between the two concepts: according to *Qǐyè bàn shèhuì* enterprises were responsible only toward employees and their families. CSR on the contrary, expand corporate responsibilities over employees, to consumers, creditors, suppliers, governments and society as a whole.

The final step of the reform cut off the social service burdens, handing them over to local governments, and transformed SOEs in modern enterprises,

[53] Ma (2010), p.125
[54] Lin (2010), p.86

specialized on their core business. However, their setting-free from social services does not mean that SOEs are exempted from undertaking social responsibilities.

As already stated CSR practices in China are strictly subject to laws and regulations and are explicitly recognized in the Company Law of 2006. In 2008 the *"Guide Opinion on the Social Responsibility Implementation for the State-Owned Enterprises Controlled by the Central Government"* , from now on called "the Guide", was released by the State-Owned Asset Supervision and Administration Commission of the State Council (SASAC). At the present time there are about one hundred fifty SOEs directly subject to government's control and most of them are large enterprises listed on the Shanghai or Shenzhen Stock Exchanges[55]. The importance of CSR for SOEs is explained in the first part of the Guide Opinion: CSR promotes social harmony and SOEs are at the base of China's economy, affecting all aspects of Chinese people's lives. CSR should therefore be implemented by SOEs to meet public expectations, to assure harmony and stability. CSR practices are moreover considered of fundamental importance for a sustainable development, which is an urgent topic in China. As a last point, the Guide Opinion affirms that CSR is a necessity for SOEs *"to participate in the international market and society"*[56]. SOEs are supposed to integrate CSR practices in their corporate structure, focusing on the majority of the common topics of international CSR standards: compliance with laws and honesty, increase profitability, improve quality, environmental protection and efficient management of resources, production safety, innovation, employees' legal rights and, lastly, charitable contributions.

---

[55] Lin (2010), p.73
[56] Id

In order to effectively integrate CSR practices into business models, the Guide Opinion suggests a series of quite vague means of implementation: "*cultivate a culture*" of CSR by educating employees, including CSR in strategies and corporate governance, for instance by establishing a CSR management. It prescribes moreover to issue periodic CSR reports or sustainability reports. CSR practices in SOEs should be preached by the organs of the Chinese Communist Party who are actively involved in the enterprises' structures and corporate governances.

According to SASAC, "*the CSR principles for the Chinese SOEs should be consistent with the international trend but also be compatible with the national and organizational reality in China*"[57].

[57] Lin (2010), p.74

Part III - The Sichuan earthquake

3.1 General Overview

On May 12, 2008 a deadly earthquake hit the province of Sichuan (四川, *Sìchuān*) in the southwestern part of China measuring at 7.98 M_s and killing an estimated 70.000 people[58]. The natural disaster became famous as the Great Sichuan Earthquake (四川大地震, *Sìchuān dà dìzhèn)* or as the Wenchuan Earthquake (汶川大地震, *Wènchuān dà dìzhèn*) as the epicenter was located in the Wenchuan County, 80 km northwest from the capital of the province Chengdu (成都, *Chéngdū*). Tremors were felt as far away as Beijing, Shanghai and Taiwan, causing landslides, power failures and fallen mobile phone towers[59]. According to reports of the Red Cross and of state officials, the earthquake left about 15 million people displaced, 5 million of which homeless and other 18.000 people were listed as missing[60]. The Sichuan Earthquake has been recorded as the deadliest earthquake that hit China since the 1976 Tangshan Earthquake and as the 21st deadliest earthquake of all time. During the months after the disaster the entire area was hit by strong aftershocks, some of those with a magnitude of 6 M_s, which caused new casualties and made the rescue efforts even more difficult. The latest aftershock measuring more than 6 M_s occurred on August 5, 2008.

---

[58] Data retrieved from http://earthquake.usgs.gov/earthquakes/eqinthenews/2008/us2008ryan/#summary

[59] Hooker, J. And Yardley, J. (2008, May 13). Powerful quake ravages China, killing thousand. New York Times

[60] http://www.ifrc.org

The direct economic loss estimated reached a top of 845 billion RMB [61] (US$121.536.000.000). Economics planners were faced with the greatest problem of maintaining the strict policies previously implemented in the province in order to avoid the economic bubble deriving from the over-investment in fixed assets while funding the reconstruction of affected areas.

The province of Sichuan is the major supplier of grain and rice for entire China and has been historically known as “Province of Abundance”, being a top producer of cereals, pork and silkworm cocoons. Statistically, Sichuan’s arable land counts for the 8.2 percent of the nation's and supplies the national grain market for the 9.2 percent[62]. Agricultural output is 8 percent point higher than the national average, and it makes up about 20 percent of Sichuan's GDP. In recent years the economy of the province has faced also an increase of the industry sector, in particular of heavy industry regarding coal, energy, iron and steel. The earthquake severely affected the economic performance of the province in 2008: the development of the tourism industry, for instance, was dampened and met a 10.3 percent decline in revenue in 2008[63]. Experts feared that the disaster would have worsened inflation, as grain and pork are two of the strongest inflationary forces in China.

"The earthquake, while not affecting a huge amount of output, will slow the ramping up of food supply and postpone a fall in prices, as well as add pressure to non-food CPI inflation once reconstruction starts," says Lehman Brothers

[61] Data source: http://www.shanghaidaily.com/, http://rbc.cn
[62] Information available at http://news.xinhuanet.com
[63] Data available at http://www.starmass.com/china_review/provincial_overview/sichuan_demographic_economy.htm

analyst Sun Mingchun. "The earthquake could exacerbate panic over rice supply problems, given shortages in the global market."[64]

On May 21, 2008 Premier Wen Jiabao announced that 70 billion Yuan (10.1 billion US dollars) would have been allocated in 2008 as fund for reconstruction of quake-hit regions.

"On the one hand, we must continue rescue and relief efforts; on the other, we must promote the sound and rapid development of society and the economy" said Premier Wen.

3.2 Companies' Response

After the earthquake the response of national and foreign companies was immediate. Half of the listed firms on the Chinese Stock Exchange got involved in the fund raising, both through cash donations and through goods and services contributions. The China Charity Foundation (CFF) defined as "extraordinary" both the number of companies participating and the amount of donations.

The US-China Business Council (USCBC) developed and maintained a list of donations of US companies and of members of the Council[65]. Among them, 3M made a donation of 1.1 million RMB (US$157.000) in cash and 3.05 million RMB (US$435.000) in medical and security material, receiving consequently an award for its involvement in the rescue effort. The Boeing Company, together with Shenzhen Airlines, launched a project called "Flight of Hope"[66] which delivered tons of medical supplies to Chengdu[67]. Cisco and Intel China, both

---

[64] Sun Minchung interviewed by Xinhua on May 29, 2008

[65] List available at https://www.uschina.org/public/china/2008/earthquake_contributions.html

[66] Boeing News release on June 19, 2008. Available at http://www.boeing.com/news/releases/2008/q2/080619a_nr.html

[67] By means of a new Boeing 737

recognized and awarded for their Corporate Social Responsibility practices in 2008, actively supported the reconstruction of schools and helped restoring phone and Internet connections in the province of Sichuan. Several MNCs encouraged its employees to make personal donations[68] .

Generally speaking, many MNCs pursued a global CSR policy in line with international standards. As the permissions for the donation were to be sent to headquarters around the world, in the immediate aftermath of the event MNCs were not as fast as their Chinese counterpart in cooperating actively to the relief efforts. By May 20, Chinese companies had outshone foreign companies in donating cash and goods.

"The popular perception was that international firms' relief contributions not only did not match those of local Chinese companies in terms of scale or timeliness, but also were not commensurate with their presence in the Chinese market"[69].

3.3 International Iron Roosters

Multinational companies that chose to follow an international standard, without taking into account the particular mentality and perceptions of Chinese consumers, got harshly criticized and came to be called "iron roosters". This term is derived from a Chinese idiom that states the impossibility for a rooster made of iron of giving even a single feather and refers therefore to a "stingy" subject who is reluctant when it comes to giving his money. A list titled *international iron roosters* circulated immediately after the earthquake via text messages, e-mail, on forums and chats among Chinese consumers, urging into

[68] Ford Motor Company (500.000 RMB, US$72.000), Hewlett-Packard (US$350.000), IBM (3 million RMB, US$430,000)
[69] Taken from article published on April 20, 2009. Available at http://knowledge.wharton.upenn.edu/article.cfm?articleid=2213

boycotting the iron roosters and into excluding them from the Chinese market. The majority of the companies listed had donated less than 5 million RMB (approx. US$720.000) in their initial rescue efforts, much less than the 10 million RMB (approx. US$1.440.000) that Chinese consumers considered “acceptable”. On the top of the list was Samsung, followed by Nokia, Daikin, LV, Coca Cola and McDonald’s. One of the roosters was KFC Corporation, the world's most popular American chicken restaurant chain. Its many stores in the Sichuan area were besieged and prevented from conducting business. On May 20, 2008 a McDonald’s restaurant was assaulted by a hundred people protesting the lack of donations of the company. MNCs responded applying to headquarters for further donations and in two weeks after the publishing of the list all companies increased the amount of donations over the edge of 10 million RMB. Nokia upped its donation from 3 to 10 million RMB, Coca Cola from 5 to 17 million RMB and KFC from 3 to 20 million RMB[70].

An important Chinese company appeared on the list among MNCs. The top Chinese real estate brand, the Vanke Company, contributed to the relief efforts donating 2 million RMB (US$295.000), considered not enough by the public opinion for such a rich and successful enterprise. Its chairman Wang Shi got harshly criticized, among the others for his millionaire income of the previous year, and was forced to publicly apologize for the scarcity of contributions. One month after the disaster Vanke published a statement about its earthquake donations and its decision of increasing the amount previously set.

Consequently to the publication of the list, public opinion chose to support Chinese companies involved in the collection of funds. An illustrative example is the relatively small Chinese company producing soft drinks, whose parent group

[70] Article published on April 20, 2009. Available at http://knowledge.wharton.upenn.edu/article.cfm?articleid=2213

Hangzhou JDB Beverage Corporation (杭州加多宝饮料有限公司, *Jiaduobao*) immediately after the disaster donated 100 million RMB (approx. US$14.5 million) during the CCTV disaster gala relief[71], increasing its popularity among consumers beyond any expectation. In the months following the disaster the JDB group could not face the booming demand for its products, in particular for Wong Lo Kat, an herbal ice tea. Wong Lo Kat (王老吉, known as *Wanglaoji* in mainland China) began to show up in all sorts of sales channels and on every single shelf of supermarkets all over the country.

Consumers' willingness to support Chinese companies is well represented by the doggerel that circulated in the months following the earthquake:

"In the future drink Wanglaoji (100 million RMB), save your money at the Industrial and Commerce Bank (87.26 million RMB), use China Mobile phone service (58.2 million RMB), use Suning consumer electronics, use QQ IMS on the Internet, buy Xiuzheng medicine, buy Ping'an insurance, buy Lenovo computers, drive Geely cars ..."

3.4 Corporate Philanthropic Disaster Response

Starting from the 60s the occurrence of natural disasters has been constantly increasing, making the need for financial and social disaster relief efforts from government, corporations and individuals higher and higher.

Concerning corporations, Carroll (1979, 1991) developed a CSR model composed of economic, legal, ethical and philanthropic responsibilities, in which philanthropy is at the top of the pyramid but accounts for only a relatively small part. As stated by Wood (1991), "the domain of discretionary responsibility

[71] CCTV Charity gala "Contributions of Love" held on May 18, 2008

typically has been operationalized as corporate philanthropy or occasionally as corporate involvement in public-private partnerships of collaborative social problem-solving ventures". Corporate philanthropy aims at the betterment of the society over the minimum level settled by the other areas of CSR practices. It is often considered as a way of giving back the profits earned in a society for the general improvement of the whole community. This may be implemented through several channels as donations and cash contributions, employee volunteerism, sponsorships, cause-related marketing and partnerships with government or non-profit entities. Saiia *et al.* (2003) asserted that firms "do good in order to do well", defining philanthropy as the "giving of corporate resources to address non-business community issues that also benefit the firm's strategic position and, ultimately, its bottom line".

According to previous research, Chinese enterprises emphasize philanthropy and disaster relief as a priority among CSR practices. After the 2008 Sichuan earthquake, companies' response was immediate and large amount of donations were announced[72] in short times. Research has discovered a direct relation between corporate philanthropic disaster response (CPDR) and corporate ownership type among Chinese enterprises (Zhang, Rezaee, Zhu, 2009). The likelihood and extent of corporate philanthropy have been studied related to ownership type and results stressed that state-owned companies (SOEs) are less responsive if compared to private companies. The authors took as an assumption that private enterprises are likely to be more strategically motivated and therefore more stimulated in engaging in CPDR than SOEs, which in most cases are large companies with substantial monopoly power. This implies that "Chinese firms' response to corporate philanthropy is strategic and

[72] Earthquake Aid for China, May 14, 2008. Retrieved from http://in.reuters.com/article/2008/05/16/quake-aid-idINSP28061020080516

economic-driven,". Philanthropy can increase firm value and develop a better image of the company in the eyes of consumers, improving customer relations in maintaining sustainable performance. Consequently, the engagement of firms in CPDR may be seen as a mechanism for gaining strategic advantages (Zhang, Rezaee, Zhu, 2009)

In 2010 Sun (Sun, 2010) conducted a study on how Chinese and multinational companies responded to the 2008 earthquake and what kind of CPDR strategy they followed. Based on a sample of 45 multinational companies and 23 Chinese companies chosen according to specific requirements[73], the study analyzed official releases from firms' online news center or new archives. Data were collected in a 14-month period between May 2008 and July 2009. In order to examine the CPDR online, releases were categorized by purpose (i.e. message contained), corporate involvement (i.e. relief action or effort undertaken) and partnership with external entities. Results showed that the majority (72.1%) of the companies chose web-based releases to communicate corporate efforts and that the same channel was preferred for encouraging help, for expressing sorrow, for promoting business recovery and expressing concern for employees.

The most commonly adopted forms of contributions were monetary and in-kind donations (40.1% and 17.8%, respectively), whereas cause-related marketing was mentioned only in the 2.3% of the press releases examined. Business-related services and long-term programs were other two quite frequently selected CPDR practices.

[73] Whether they were conducting their business in China and whether they had a signature website in Chinese language

The study highlighted significant differences between MNCs and Chinese companies, both in the communication techniques and in the practices implemented. Firstly, MNCs present higher percentages of press releases online than Chinese firms. Both parts published the majority of releases in May 2008, immediately after the occurrence of the disaster and sharply decreased the number in the following months, "revealing the disaster relief activities as ad hoc corporate philanthropy"[74]. However, MNCs focused on long-term programs more than local counterparts. This reflects the standard practice of CSR in Western countries and it is clear expression of the belief that stakeholder "tend to view longer-term contributions (...) as expressing genuine concern for a cause". Another similarity showed by the study was the purpose of the press release: both local enterprises (85.7%) and foreign companies (95.8%) had chosen the release as a way of communicating and publicizing corporate efforts. Cash and goods donations were the primary form of involvement from both parts, however Chinese companies reported a higher percentage of employee donations. This reflects the influence that Chinese culture and the values of the Communist Party have on CSR practices of Chinese firms. Many Chinese companies defined employee donations as a collectivistic action. As asserted by previous research, the affiliation to China's Communist party implies caring for others, and the 2008 disaster response is an illustrative example of how deeply this way of thinking is rooted among Chinese people.

The greatest difference pointed out by the analysis was the total absence of supplementary information [75] in the releases of Chinese firms. Many multinationals, on the contrary, reported more figures and facts about the company, about its CSR practices and about its other operations in China.

[74] Dongran, S. (2010), p. 33

[75] Company introduction, links to other related websites and materials and contact information

MNCs, furthermore, were more likely to mention their cooperation with external organizations as non-profit organizations, governments and other business units. Tang et al. (2008) argued that multinationals were trying to communicate their growing legitimacy and acceptance in the Chinese market.

"Philanthropic disaster response communication is different from other CSR communications because increased media focus and public inspection over a short period of time amplify company's actions and gestures taken after disasters"[76].

As a consequence, a proper corporate philanthropic disaster response practice is of fundamental importance within a firm CSR program. Apart from the more philanthropic point of view about the betterment of society, corporate disaster response has proved itself as an effective way of promoting the company's image and appealing to consumers and therefore as an alternative way of doing business and enhancing profits. A disaster response policy should be planned independently from disaster occurring and should be considered as an essential aspect of CSR practices within the company, to be integrated strategically into the business model.

[76] Dongran, S. (2010), p. 43

Part IV - From theory to reality

The China National Petroleum Corporation, presented previously, is a large Chinese SOE working in an international environment, and therefore subject to the most different trends and currents of thought concerning CSR practices.

4.1 CNPC and SOEs

Despite the reform of SOEs, the Chinese government kept its control over the more crucial sectors of electricity supply, telecommunications, transportation system, finance and banking and coal and petroleum supply. As a Chinese state-owned company operating in the field of oil upstream operations, the CNPC has to meet specific state regulations, among them the Company Law of 2006 and the Guide of 2008. These laws regulate CSR practices determining the social duties of the company and suggesting ways to implement adequate policies. The CNPC's efforts towards the creation of an harmonious development of the company within the society corresponds perfectly to the main aim of the 2008 Guide, which preaches social harmony and sustainable development as the base of Chinese economy[77]. Many other parallelisms are to be found between the CSR statements of CNPC and the law, most of the times through the usage of same words and expressions.
The Guide prescribes moreover to SOEs to actively participate in the international market, on the one hand to boost Chinese economy at international levels, on the other to finally abandon the concept of SOEs as a typical Chinese governmental body[78]. This implies, among the others, that the company has to meet several international regulations and certifications in addition to domestic

[77] See 2.6
[78] Id.

ones. With its business operations in more than 20 foreign countries, CNPC has achieved the goal of quitting the role of mere supplier of social service in China and has confirmed itself as a successful international player compatibly with the national reality, without dropping common Chinese standards and still maintaining some governmental administrative functions, which are however never specified in detail.

4.2 CNPC and Chinese CSR

According to Matten and Moon, China is supposed to develop an implicit form of corporate social responsibility, in which practices are set by regulations and are perceived as an obligation for the company and not as a discretional instrument. Following a collectivistic trend, companies operating within an implicit CSR framework are more likely to implement systemic practices, driven by the institutions[79]. The case of CNPC partially confirms this trend foreseen by Matten and Moon. As a state-owned company, indeed, CNPC is subject to specific regulations concerning CSR practices and CSR disclosures, with the already mentioned aim of an harmonious relationship with the society as a whole. The corporation, however, being actively involved in the international market, has followed a peculiar pattern, starting to implement more international CSR practices and therefore getting closer to an explicit form of social responsibility, as an isolated actor following discretionary policies. The research conducted by Sun in 2010, for instance, highlighted some differences in corporate philanthropic disaster response practices among multinationals and Chinese companies. According to the result of the research, Chinese companies concentrated their efforts in the period immediately following the disaster, choosing employee donations as the most important form of contribution and

[79] See 2.2

avoiding the spreading of supplementary information about the company itself. CNPC presents the same behavior concerning employees donation and different types of message spread, however it has, as many multinational enterprises, involved in long-term programs and publicized its cooperation with other companies or governmental bodies[80]. This may be seen as the concrete fact that even a Chinese SOEs can get closer to international standards, creating a mixture of domestic and foreign CSR principles. On the other hand, CNPC presents typical Chinese CSR dimensions: good faith is repeatedly reported as an essential principle of CNPC social involvement. Employment, listed by the research of Xu as a unique Chinese CSR dimension[81], is one of the main objectives declared by the corporation, together with social stability and progress. As for as the majority of Chinese companies, the corporation does not mention shareholders or equality issues among its CSR practices, preferring environment, safety, health and public welfare instead. The latter, in particular, reflects the conceptual framework of Chinese corporate social responsibility practices elaborated according to Chinese cultural principles and characteristics, among which collectivism and Confucianism were enumerated, which cause Chinese corporate social responsibility practices to differ, sometimes even significantly, from Western ones.

[80] See 1.5
[81] See 2.4

Conclusions

This thesis aimed at investigating the development of corporate social responsibility practices in China, both by reviewing the existing literature on CSR and the Chinese reality and by observing the CSR model integrated into a real Chinese enterprise.

In this concluding part, the results of the research are presented and, hopefully, an answer will be given to the two questions proposed initially.

Are cultural and historical factors relevant in the creation and development of the Chinese CSR model?

In order to answer this question, the historical and economic background of China has been explored, starting from the creation of the People's Republic of China in 1949 and then going through the Economic Reform that took place in the 1970s. A general overview of the existing legislation, in particular of the Company Law of 2006 and the Guide of 2008 was given, highlighting the differences existing between private and state-owned enterprises, both in role covered and in obligations set by law.. Regulations make clear how to intend corporate social responsibility, suggest ways to integrate it into business models and attempt to make CSR a regular practice among companies, requiring for instance annual reports and declarations. Moreover, an analysis of the philosophical and cultural principles which may affect the market in China has been carried out, focusing on concepts which are commonly knew as deeply rooted into the everyday life of Chinese people. According to hypotheses, the cultural and social background should be reflected into the way companies conduct their business, and therefore in the way they construct their CSR models.

We saw that Confucianism, considered the cornerstone of Chinese culture, suggest the direction that CSR practices have to follow: society and relationships within it have to develop in an harmonious way. The same expression “harmonious” is to be found in the 2008 Guide as well as in the CNPC CSR declaration. According to Zhu and Yao, the five principles of *ren* has shaped the modern value of CSR and “*invisibly formed the fundamental sources of modern CSR”* . As an example, the unique dimension of CSR of operating in good faith, observed by Xu *et al.*, directly reflects the *xin* principle, which prescribes to act in an honest way in everyday actions.

Collectivism on the other hand, considered a typical characteristic of the Chinese culture, can obviously be linked to the attention that Chinese enterprises pay for the common development and betterment of society. *Social stability and progress* figured among the unique dimensions spotted by Xu *et al.*, without a counterpart in the Western CSR model and, in line with Xu’s research, the CNPC listed explicitly “employment” as a target of its CSR practices.

In addition, the different applications of Corporate Philanthropic Disaster Response after the Sichuan earthquake may be analyzed under the perspective of different cultural principles between Chinese companies and MNCs. The way Chinese enterprises chose to spread their messages of sorrow and their commitment to the relief efforts differed from the Western ones’. This may be due to the concept of low/high-context society, considering Asian cultures as high-context, where a great importance is given to the message itself. Furthermore, the incredible amount of employee donations and volunteering reached by Chinese firms against Western ones, underlines the idea of a collectivistic society, in which group welfare is more important than the individual, and stresses the importance that Chinese people give to cohesion and interdependence among social groups.

In conclusion, it may be possible to find a direct relation between the cultural (and historical) background and the development of a specific corporate social responsibility sensibility. Cultural concepts influence, sometimes not perceptibly, the way a nation thinks, sees the surrounding reality, perceives events and situations and, therefore, influences society's reactions and behavior. As a consequence, it is obvious to presume that business models and therefore CSR practices will be formed according to the dominant cultural framework.

Is it possible, for a Chinese company, to combine the peculiarities of Chinese CSR with the international and Western CSR concepts?

This question was partly answered in part IV, through the comparison of the expected CSR model of a Chinese company, the actual model implemented by CNPC and the Western concept of social responsibility. Similarities and unique factors have been highlighted concerning CNPC. On the one hand the corporation adheres to the most typical Chinese CSR concepts, as the harmonious development of business operations, the attention given to the collectivity and the pursue of a good faith-driven behavior in everyday business operations. On the other hand however, due to the several international relationships undertaken, the corporation had to adapt to international standards, embracing the typical MNCs' conduct. As an example of that, CNPC's disaster relief efforts after the Sichuan earthquake are in some aspects similar to those of multinational companies. This may be the clear sign that a Chinese enterprise, even a state-owned one, may choose to follow international CSR practices, combining them with the national model. This is actually a necessity for companies operating in an international context, as the increasing globalization of markets urges players to adapt and standardize their conduct, both to be accepted in the market and to be at the same level of competitors. In an era in which media play a dominant role in building the image of a company at a global level, an adequate CSR policy gets to be a fundamental tool to integrate into the business model. However, as shown by the example of CNPC, for a company it is possible to combine international and domestic CSR principles, as one dimension does not necessarily eliminate the other.

Limitations and future perspectives

Several limitations are to be acknowledged to this study. Firstly, only big enterprises have been taken into consideration, omitting to analyze current CSR declarations of small enterprises. CNPC is as a matter of fact a multinational player, therefore "biased" towards an international direction. It would be interesting to analyze the CSR model of a small Chinese enterprise which does not have contacts outside China, whose CSR practices are probably undergoing a different pattern of development as subject to different impulses. Secondly, market and consumer reactions have been neglected. These have however a great impact on the establishment and on the development of a CSR model, in particular in a country where corporate social responsibility is a quite new issue.

In recent year, corporate social responsibility in China has received ever increasing attention by media and scholars. Different kinds of investigations were conducted, some focusing on the dimensions of CSR, others on the current legislation, others on the differences with the Western model, others on the internal division between SOEs and private companies. As already stated, however, the Sichuan earthquake has deeply affected the development of a CSR sensibility throughout China and it would be interesting to see whether the international media coverage, which actually started effectively only in 2008, has really influenced the trend in the following years. It would be moreover fascinating to investigate whether the increasing globalization is going to lead to a diminishing presence of unique CSR dimensions among different countries.

Bibliography

Books

Hofstede, G. (2002). *Culture's consequences: Comparing values, behaviors, institutions, and organizations across nations* (2. ed.) Thousand Oaks.

Yao, X. (2000). *An introduction to Confucianism*. United Kingdom: Cambridge University Press.

Academic Articles

Campbell, J. L. (2007). *Why would corporations behave in socially responsible ways? An institutional theory of Corporate Social Responsibility*. The Academy of Management Review, 32(3), 946-967

Carroll, A. B. (1991). *The pyramid of corporate social responsibility: Toward the moral management of organizational stakeholders*. Business and Society, 38(3), 39 - 48

Carroll, A. B. (1979). *A three-dimensional conceptual model of corporate performance*. The Academy of Management Review, 4(4), 497-505

Committee for Economic Development (1971). *Social responsibilities of business corporations*

Dongran, S. (2010). *Communicating corporate social responsibility: Corporate philanthropic disaster response after the 2008 Sichuan earthquake in china*. University of Miami

Li Wen, L. (2010). *Corporate Social Responsibility in China: Window dressing or structural change?* Berkeley Journal of International Law, 28(1), 64-100

Ma, D. (2006). *Tocquevillian moments: Charitable contributions by Chinese private entrepreneurs.* Social Forces, 85(2), 943-964

Ma, Z. (2010). *The SINS in business negotiations: Explore the cross-cultural differences in business ethics between Canada and China.* Journal of Business Ethics, , 123-135

Matten, D. (2008). *"Implicit" and "Explicit" CSR: a conceptual framework for a comparative understanding of Corporate Social Responsibility.* The Academy of Management Review, 33(2), 404-424

Moon, J., & Shen, X. (2010). *CSR in china research: Salience, focus and nature.* Journal of Business Ethics, 94(4), 613-629

Ramasamy, B. (2004). *A comparative analysis of corporate social responsibility awareness.* Journal of Corporate Citizenship, (13), 109-123

Saiia, D., Carroll, A., & Buchholtz, A. (2003). *Philanthropy as strategy.* Business Society, 42(2), 169

Sarkis, J., Ni, N., & Zhu, Q. (2011). *Winds of Change: Corporate Social Responsibility in China.* Ivey Business Journal, 75(1), 1-1

Shen, S., & Cheng, H. (2009). *Economic globalization and the construction of china's corporate social responsibility.* International Journal of Law and Management, 51(3), 134-138

Shujie, Y., Jianling, W., & Ling, S. (2010). *Is market reactions and corporate philantrophy: A case study of the Wenchuan earthquake in china.* The University of Nottingham - China Policy Institute.

Wood, D. J. (1991). *Corporate social performance revisited.* The Academy of Management Review, 16(4), pp. 691-718. Retrieved from http://www.jstor.org/stable/258977

Xu, S. (2010). *Indigenous characteristics of Chinese Corporate Social Responsibility conceptual paradigm.* Journal of Business Ethics, 93(2), 321-333

Yang, Z., & Wang, C. L. (2011). *Guanxi as a governance mechanism in business markets: Its characteristics, relevant theories, and future research directions.* Industrial Marketing Management, 40(4), 492-495

Yingbi, F. (2010). *Corporate social responsibility in China: A study on Corporate Social Responsibility for multinational corporations in China.* (Capstone Thesis, American University).

Zhang, R., Rezaee, Z., & Zhu, J. (2010). *Corporate philanthropic disaster response and ownership type: Evidence from Chinese firms' response to the Sichuan earthquake.* Journal of Business Ethics, 91(1), 51-63

Zhu, W., & Yao, Y. (2008). *On the value of traditional Confucian culture and the value of modern Corporate Social Responsibility.* International Journal of Business and Management, 3(2), 58 – 62

Web Sources

http://www.cnpc.com.cn

http://en.cnki.com.cn/

http://www.chinacsrmap.com

http://www.szse.cn

http://www.csr-china.net

http://www.amcham-shanghai.org

http://www.cntv.cn/

http://knowledge.ckgsb.edu.cn/

http://www.wbcsd.org

http://www.sasac.gov.cn

http://www.syntao.com/

http://earthquake.usgs.gov